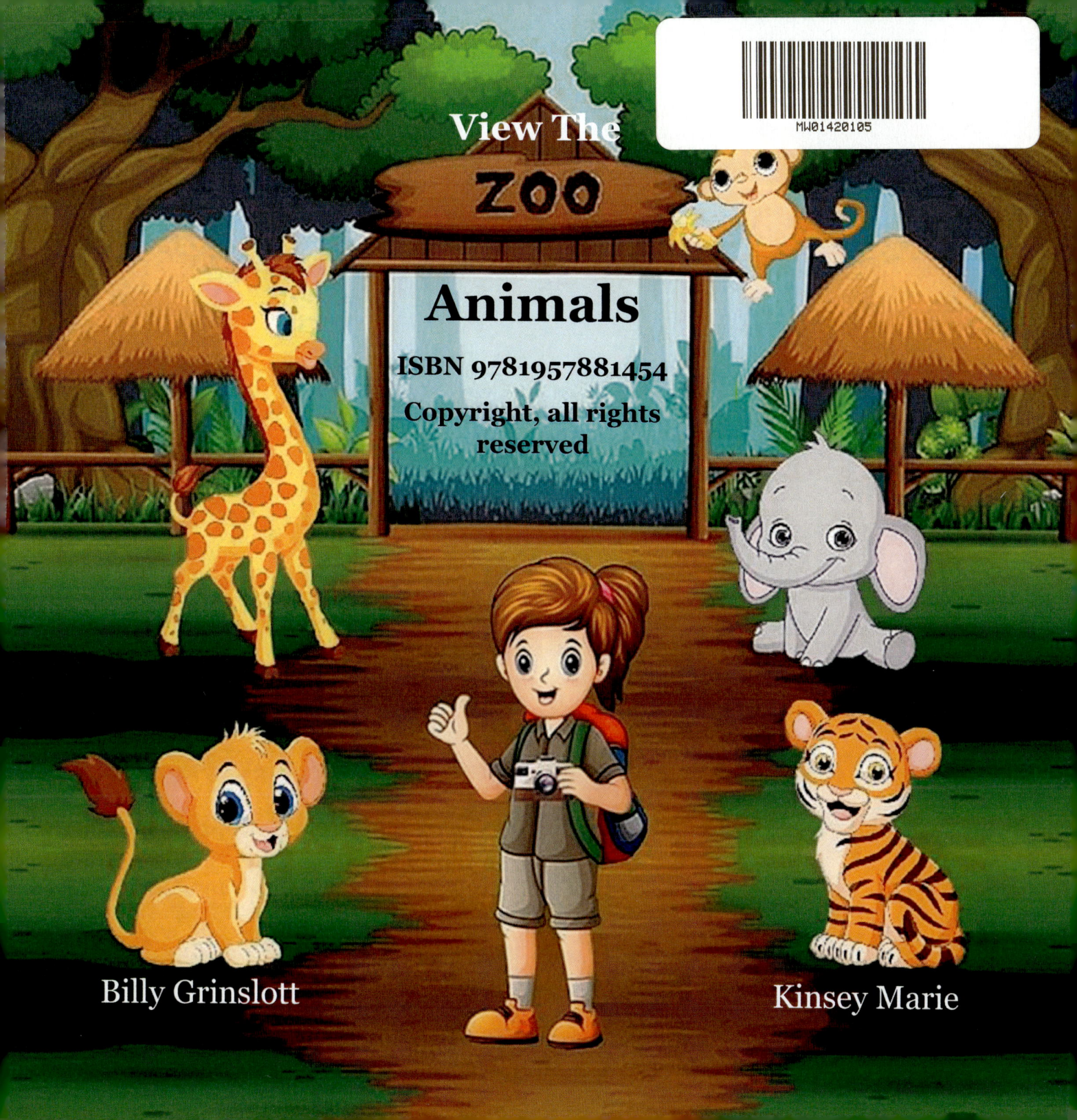

In the Amphibian section at the zoo, there are different frogs. Frogs have excellent night vision and are very sensitive to movement. Frogs were the first land animals with vocal cords we call it a croak. The bull frog has a loud croak.

You will see many reptiles at the zoo. Some of them include the lizard family like Iguanas, Gila monsters and many more of the lizard family. Lizards come in all sizes and colors and are cool to look at.

There are many turtles on display at the zoo. The most popular are the Galapagos turtles. They're the biggest tortoises in the world. They're also the oldest. They can live for a year without food or water. They like taking naps.

There are many different types of snakes at the zoo. The boa constrictor is one of the more popular ones. They get their name because they wrap themselves around other animals and trees. They have a lot of strength and can crush whatever they wrap around. It's best not to let a boa constrictor wrap around you, because they can hurt you.

The anaconda is another popular snake. Anacondas are the world's largest snake. It can grow up to 30 feet long, about as long as your school bus. A full-grown anaconda can weigh up to 550 pounds. Anacondas are constrictors. They kill their prey by squeezing it to death just like a boa constrictor.

Some other critters you might see at the zoo are otters and beavers. Otters are clever creatures, they'll use rocks to crack open the clams. Beavers have a flat tail they use to slap on the water when they are frightened. Beavers like to chew down trees and build dams that they can live in. Beavers are powerful swimmers that can swim underwater for up to 15 minutes.

Many zoos exhibit seals. The smallest seal is the Galapagos seal the largest is the elephant seal. Seals can sleep underwater. Seals can dive up to 2000 feet. Seals can be hooligans, they like to have fun and are very friendly. Mother seals and pups bond with a unique call. Their brain temperature drops when they dive, to protect their brain from swimming in cold water.

Sea Lions and seals like to have fun. Many zookeepers train sea lions and seals to fetch balls and other toys. Sea lions and seals are very social and can be taught tricks.

Here's some members of the dog family that are at the zoo. On the left is a wolf, in the center is a fox and on the right is a coyote. Foxes are very vocal and make 40 different sounds. Foxes have impeccable hearing. Foxes are extremely playful. Coyotes communicate with a yipping call.

The wolf is one of the biggest members of the dog family. They have a loud howl that sends chills down your spine. The timber wolf is the biggest of all the wolves. Pups are born deaf and blind with bright blue eyes until they mature.

There are many cats at the zoo. In the northern zoos, they may have a snow leopard. Snow Leopards are used to living in colder climates. They can't roar like other big cats. They wrap their tail around their head and neck and use it as a scarf for warmth. Their paws are huge and make good snowshoes for traveling in the snow.

Some of the other cats that zoos have are black panthers on the left, Bobcats in the center and cougars, on the right, otherwise known as mountain lions. Mountain lions, pumas, and cougars are all the same species. Mountain lions are the biggest of these cats and live just about everywhere in America.

Flamingos get their pink color from their food.

Flamingos are filter feeders and turn their heads upside down to eat. A group of flamingo's is called a flamboyance.

There are many different types of birds at the zoo. There will be domestic and tropical birds. The most common ones are Parrots, eagles, ducks, peacock's, falcons, owls, cranes, pelicans, toucans, ostriches and emus.

The body of Dall sheep is covered with a white woolly coat that provides protection against low temperatures. Both males and females have horns. Their horns take up to 8 years to grow. The age of the sheep can be calculated from the number of growth rings on their horns. Dall sheep spend most of their lives on the jagged slopes of mountains. Their cloven hooves with rough pads help them cling to cliff edges and ledges.

What are those large animals? Ones got long hair and a beard and the other one doesn't. That is a Bison with the long hair and beard. The other one is a Buffalo. Bison and Buffalo sometimes are confused as the same animal. But as you can see, they look completely different. Only Bison have long hair.

Caribou are also known as reindeer, they are the same animal. Both male and female reindeer grow antlers, Reindeer are covered in hair from their nose to the bottom of their hooves. Reindeer are the only deer species to have hair completely covering their nose. Reindeer are the only deer species to be widely domesticated. Santa uses Reindeer to pull his slay. Rudolph the reindeer is the most popular of the reindeer.

Kudu are the largest member of the antelope family. They produce one of the loudest sounds made by antelope in the form of a gruff bark like a dog. Kudus have long horns with spirals that help protect them from other animals. Kudus are highly alert and hard to approach. Only male Kudus have horns that continue to grow, and they never lose them. Kudus are fast and can jump high.

There may some types of deer at the zoo. The whitetail deer is the most popular deer in North America. A male deer is called a buck, a female is a doe, and a baby is called a fawn. Whitetail deer have good eyesight and hearing. Many zoos will let you feed corn to the deer.

Some zoos will have Guanaco, Alpacas or Llamas. Llamas are excellent guardians. Llamas have sharp eyes and ears and are quite intelligent. Llamas are known for spitting at other animals and even humans. So be careful when approaching one, it may spit at you.

The sloth gets its name because it moves really slow. Sloths move so slowly that algae and fungi have time to land and grow on them. Sloths are blind. They are faster in water than on land. It takes sloths 30 days to digest their food because their metabolism is so slow. They are 3 times stronger than humans.

Orangutans are the biggest and heaviest tree-dwelling animal. They've got long arms. They eat with their feet. They build nests to sleep in. Some orangutans use sticks and rocks as tools.

There are many monkeys and chimpanzees at the zoo. The most popular is the spider monkey. Spider monkeys have strong tails and can hang from them. They Don't Have Thumbs like other monkeys. They are swinging specialists. They are social animals and like to hang out in groups.

Gorillas have hands and feet like humans including thumbs and big toes. Some gorillas in captivity have learned to use sign language to communicate with humans. Gorillas pound their chest as a type of communication. People share around 98% of our DNA with gorillas. They are one of the biggest, most powerful living primates. They have 16 different types of calls. Gorillas live in small groups called troops or bands.

Quack, Quack, Quack. What are those birds that are floating on the water? They are ducks. Look there's also a frog sitting on a rock. Ducks can float and have webbed feet to help them swim. Their feathers repel water, so they don't get wet. Baby ducks are called ducklings, a male is a drake, and a female is a hen.

The ostrich has the longest legs and neck of any bird species. Ostriches can't fly even though they have wings. They run instead of flying. With their long legs they can run up to 45 miles per hour. Ostrich's legs are strong, and they can front kick other animals. Ostriches live in small flocks and check their eggs by sticking their head into the hole where their eggs are. Ostriches like water and enjoy taking baths.

Some zoos will have penguins you can see. Even though penguins have what looks like wings, they are actually flippers they use to swim with. The emperor penguin is the largest penguin. Penguins like to huddle together when its cold out. They also like sliding in the snow. Penguins are excellent swimmers and divers.

The Polar Bear is the biggest bear on earth. Male polar bears can weigh up to 1500 lbs. They like swimming and can swim constantly for days at a time. Polar bears keep warm thanks to the blubber under their skin. They can smell up to a mile away. They can run 25 mph and swim up to 10mph.

Puffins are also nicknamed sea parrots or clowns of the see. Because their big orange beak looks like a parrots or clown's nose. A puffin's beak changes color during the year. In spring it blooms with an outrageous orange color. When flying, Puffins flap their wings up to 400 times a minute and fly up to 55 mph. They are also great swimmers. Their downy feathers make them appear puffed up, that's how they got their name Puffins.

Bald Eagles are very adaptive and live in just about every part of the world including the arctic regions. The largest bald eagles live in Alaska. They build the largest nest of any North American bird. The bald eagle is America's national bird. The bald eagle gets their name due to their white hair on their head. They can fly up to 30 mph, and dive at speeds up to 100 mph. Male bald eagles are smaller than females. Eagles return to same nesting territory year after year.

You might see an alligator at the zoo. Alligators are very social reptiles and prefer to live in groups called congregation. They are excellent and fast swimmers. Alligators are reptiles. Alligators will eat just about anything.

In the under-water world at the zoo, you can see seals, different types of fish and other creatures. But the most fun one to watch are the dolphins. They are very playful, and many zookeepers can train them to do tricks. Some dolphins will fetch a ball like a dog does. They are fun to watch.

Many zoos will have bears on exhibit. Not only can you see a polar bear, but some zoos have black bears, brown bears or grizzly bears. Brown bears are the most widely spread bear across America. Bears can climb trees. Bears have excellent senses of smell, sight, and hearing. They can see in colors like you can.

Zebras are part of the horse family, but they live in the wild. Zebras have light fur and black stripes that help to camouflage them. Zebras love to eat plants and grass. New born foals, baby zebras can stand after 6 minutes. Baby zebras have brown stripes when they are born and as they mature, they turn black. A herd or group of zebras is called a dazzle.

What are those animals with long legs and necks? They are Giraffes. They are the tallest mammal on earth. Their long legs and neck help them to eat leaves from the trees. New-born baby giraffes are taller than most humans and they can stand within 30 minutes. Giraffes can sleep standing up like a horse. Giraffes are super peaceful animals, they are easy to get along with.

Elephants are the largest land animal. They have huge ears. They can grab stuff with their trunks. Elephants eat all day long. They can't jump like other animals and humans. Elephants communicate with vibrations in the ground. Baby elephants can stand within 20 minutes after birth. Elephants are very smart, they never forget anything. Elephants purr like cats as a form of communication.

Tigers are considered one of the most beautiful cats by many, because of their astonishing looks and black stripes. Tigers are the largest amongst all the wild cats. They are strong and can knock things down with one swipe of their paw. Tiger cubs are born blind until their eyes develop. Tigers live for 25 years, and they love to swim and play in the water.

These are lions. They are known as the king of the jungle because of their raw power and strength. Lions don't fear other animals. The roar of a lion can be heard 5 miles away. Lions like to live in groups known as a pride. Male lions have mains and females do not. Female lions gather most of the food and male lions protect the herd and the young cubs, baby lions.

Author Page
View the Zoo Animals
Copyright, All Rights Reserved

Thanks

ISBN 9781957881454

To Check Out More Our Kids Books.

Visit Kinsey Marie Books or Billy Grinslott.